Witch Pu$$y

MANIFESTATION WORKBOOK

Unleash Your Devine Feminine Power

Spicy Red

Copyright© 2024 by Spicy Red.
All rights reserved.

Contents

Introduction 1

Chapter One
Understanding Your Chakras 2

Chapter Two
Connecting with Your Devine Feminine Energy 6

Chapter Three
Healing and Releasing Trauma 12

Chapter Four
Manifestation Techniques 15

Chapter Five
Affirmations and Journaling 18

Chapter Six
Rituals and Candle Magic 23

Chapter Seven
Embracing Your Journey 27

Conclusion 31

Introduction

Welcome to the Witch Pu$$y Manifestation Workbook, a transformative guide designed to help you tap into your divine feminine energy, heal, and manifest the life of your dreams. This workbook is crafted with love and intention to help women like you in harnessing the potent energies of the sacral and root chakras. Through a series of empowering exercises, you will unlock your inner power, work through traumas, and manifest your deepest desires.

— *Spicy Red*

Chapter One
Understanding Your Chakras

1.1
INTRODUCTION TO THE SACRAL AND ROOT CHAKRAS

Welcome to the journey of self-discovery and manifestation through the power of your chakras. In this chapter, we'll explore the first two energy centers, the Sacral Chakra and the Root Chakra, and how they play a pivotal role in your ability to manifest your dreams.

THE SACRAL CHAKRA (SVADHISTHANA)

The Sacral Chakra, located just below your navel, is associated with the element of water and is often referred to as the "seat of emotions" and the "center of creativity." This chakra governs your:

- Emotions

- Creativity
- Sensuality
- Passion

The Sacral Chakra is your source of inspiration and the driving force behind your desires. When it's balanced and vibrant, you'll find it easier to tap into your creative potential, express your emotions, and pursue your deepest passions.

THE ROOT CHAKRA (MULADHARA)

The Root Chakra, situated at the base of your spine, is closely connected to the Earth element and serves as your foundation for stability and security. It governs your:

- Sense of safety
- Survival instincts
- Connection to the physical world
- Grounding

A balanced Root Chakra provides you with a sense of security and stability, allowing you to build a solid foundation for your manifestations. When this chakra is unblocked and active, you can more effectively manifest your desires into the physical realm.

BALANCING YOUR SACRAL AND ROOT CHAKRAS

Your journey begins with understanding and balancing these two essential chakras. To activate your manifestation abilities, you must create harmony between your emotional, creative energy (Sacral Chakra) and your sense of grounding and security (Root Chakra).

EXERCISE 1.1: CHAKRA AFFIRMATIONS

Take a moment to sit in a quiet and comfortable space. Close your eyes, take a few deep breaths, and focus on the area just below your navel (Sacral Chakra) and the base of your spine (Root Chakra).

- For your Sacral Chakra, repeat the affirmation: "I embrace my creative power, and I allow my desires to flow freely."
- For your Root Chakra, repeat the affirmation: "I am grounded, safe, and secure. I trust in the process of life."

Repeat these affirmations daily, preferably in the morning or before your meditation practice. These affirmations will serve as the foundation of your energy work throughout this workbook.

As you continue through this journey, remember that balance in these chakras is key to unlocking your manifestation potential. By understanding and nurturing these energy centers, you will be better equipped to manifest the life you desire.

In the following chapters, we will delve deeper into connecting with your divine feminine energy and using it to heal and manifest. Keep an open heart and an open mind as you embark on this transformative path.

Chapter Two
Connecting with Your Devine Feminine Energy

2.1
EMBRACING YOUR FEMININE ESSENCE

Welcome to Chapter 2 of your Witch Pu$$y Manifestation journey. In this chapter, we'll delve into the essence of your divine feminine energy and how it relates to your ability to manifest your deepest desires.

THE DIVINE FEMININE ENERGY

The divine feminine energy represents the qualities traditionally associated with femininity, such as:

- Intuition
- Nurturing
- Sensuality

- Emotional depth
- Creativity
- Connection to nature

This energy is not limited to gender but is a powerful force within all of us. It complements the divine masculine energy and is essential for balance in our lives. When you embrace your divine feminine essence, you tap into a wellspring of power that can greatly enhance your manifestation journey.

EXERCISE 2.1: EMBRACING YOUR DIVINE FEMININE ESSENCE

1. Find a quiet, comfortable space where you won't be disturbed.

2. Close your eyes, take several deep breaths, and allow your body to relax.

3. Visualize a radiant, glowing ball of light in your heart center. This light represents your divine feminine energy.

4. Imagine this energy expanding and filling your entire being. Feel it embracing you with love, compassion, and creativity.

5. Reflect on how you can incorporate the qualities of the divine feminine into your daily life. How can you nurture yourself and others? How can you express your creativity? How can you trust your intuition more?

6. Journal your thoughts and intentions. Write down any insights or ideas that arise during this meditation.

By embracing your divine feminine essence, you're aligning yourself with the natural flow of life and enhancing your ability to manifest your desires. In the next section, we'll explore how your intuition, a key aspect of your feminine energy, plays a vital role in your manifestation journey.

2.2
THE POWER OF INTUITION

Welcome back to Chapter 2 of your Witch Pu$$y Manifestation journey. In this section, we will delve into the power of intuition and how it can enhance your manifestation skills. Intuition is a vital aspect of your divine feminine energy, guiding you on your path to manifesting your desires.

THE ESSENCE OF INTUITION

Intuition is your inner guidance system, a deep knowing that doesn't rely on logic or reasoning. It's the subtle whispers of your soul, guiding you toward what's right for you. Here's why intuition is essential for manifestation:

- Alignment: Your intuition connects you to your true desires and purpose, ensuring that your manifestations are in alignment with your authentic self.
- Timing: Intuition helps you recognize the right timing for your actions. It prevents you from forcing manifestations before they are ready to unfold.

- Course Correction: When you trust your intuition, you can make necessary adjustments along your manifestation journey, avoiding potential obstacles.

CULTIVATING YOUR INTUITION

Cultivating your intuition is an ongoing practice that requires trust and patience. Here are some exercises to help you tap into your intuitive abilities:

EXERCISE 2.2.1: DAILY INTUITIVE JOURNAL

Set aside a few minutes each day to journal your intuitive insights. Start with simple questions like, "What does my intuition tell me about my current desires?"

Write down any thoughts, feelings, or hunches that arise. Don't judge or analyze them; simply record them.

_____

_____

_____

Over time, review your journal entries and look for patterns or recurring themes. This will help you recognize your intuitive voice more clearly.

EXERCISE 2.2.2: QUIET MIND MEDITATION

Find a quiet space and sit comfortably.

Close your eyes and take several deep, calming breaths.

Clear your mind and focus on your breath. Imagine a still, tranquil pond within you.

As thoughts arise, let them pass like ripples on the pond's surface, gently returning your focus to your breath.

In this stillness, ask a question related to your desires or manifestations. Listen quietly for any intuitive responses or nudges.

Record any insights you receive in your manifestation journal below and in provided pages.

_____

_____

_____

_____

TRUSTING YOUR INTUITION

To harness the power of intuition, it's essential to trust it fully. Trusting your intuition means:

Believing in the validity of your intuitive insights, even if they defy logic.

Being open to subtle signs and synchronicities in your daily life.

Following your intuitive guidance with confidence and patience.

Remember, intuition is like a muscle—it becomes stronger with practice. As you continue your manifestation journey, your intuition will become a valuable ally, helping you make choices that align with your deepest desires.

In the next chapter, we will explore how healing past traumas is a vital step in your manifestation process. Trauma can block your intuitive abilities, and by addressing it, you'll open the doors to more effective manifestation.

Chapter Three
Healing and Releasing Trauma

Welcome to Chapter 3 of your Witch Pu$$y Manifestation journey. In this chapter, we'll delve into the importance of recognizing and healing past traumas to clear the path for effective manifestation. Trauma can act as a barrier to your intuitive and creative abilities, hindering your manifestation process.

UNDERSTANDING TRAUMA

Trauma can take many forms and arise from various life experiences, including:

- Childhood wounds
- Loss of a loved one
- Emotional or physical abuse
- Accidents or injuries
- Stressful life events
- Relationship challenges

Unresolved trauma can manifest as emotional pain, limiting beliefs, and blocks to your creative and intuitive abilities. To fully embrace your divine feminine energy and manifest your desires, it's essential to address and heal these wounds.

HEALING MEDITATION

We will begin the healing process with a guided meditation designed to release emotional wounds and promote inner healing. Find a quiet, comfortable space and follow these steps:

EXERCISE: HEALING MEDITATION

Sit or lie down in a comfortable position, ensuring you won't be disturbed.

Close your eyes and take a few deep breaths, inhaling positivity and exhaling any tension or negativity.

Visualize a serene, safe space. This could be a meadow, a beach, a forest, or any place where you feel calm and secure. Imagine a gentle, warm light surrounding you, providing comfort and protection.

Begin to bring to mind any past traumas or emotional wounds you wish to address. Allow these memories to surface without judgment.

Visualize these memories as heavy stones in your hands. One by one, release these stones into a flowing river or a bonfire, watching them dissolve and transform.

As each stone dissolves, affirm to yourself: "I release the pain of the past. I am free to heal and manifest my desires."

Continue this process until you feel a sense of lightness and relief.

Gradually return your awareness to the present moment, knowing that you have taken a significant step toward healing.

Journal your feelings and experiences after the meditation, recording any insights or emotions that arose.

Healing is an ongoing process, and this meditation is a powerful tool to help you release past traumas and open space for new manifestations. As you continue your journey, be patient and compassionate with yourself, knowing that healing takes time.

In the following chapter, we will explore specific manifestation techniques that leverage your newfound clarity and healing for more effective manifestation.

Continue your journey by exploring manifestation techniques in Chapter 4 of the workbook.

Chapter Four
Manifestation Techniques

Welcome to Chapter 4 of your Witch Pu$$y Manifestation journey. In this chapter, we'll explore specific manifestation techniques that will help you harness your newfound clarity and healing for more effective manifestations. By combining your divine feminine energy, intuition, and healing, you'll be well on your way to manifesting the life you desire.

VISION BOARD CREATION

A vision board is a powerful visualization tool that taps into the creative energy of your Sacral Chakra. It allows you to visually represent your dreams and desires, making them feel more tangible and achievable. Here's how to create your vision board:

Steps to Create a Vision Board

Gather magazines, images, and words that resonate with your desires.

- Find a large sheet of paper or a corkboard to serve as your canvas.

- Begin by meditating or quieting your mind. Focus on your intentions and what you wish to manifest.
- Cut out images and words that represent your desires and paste them on your board.
- Arrange the images and words in a way that visually pleases you. There's no right or wrong way to do this.
- Display your vision board in a place where you'll see it daily. Spend a few moments each day focusing on it and feeling the emotions associated with your desires.

Your vision board serves as a daily reminder of your manifestations, keeping your intentions at the forefront of your mind.

ROOT CHAKRA GROUNDING EXERCISE

Before diving into your manifestations, it's crucial to establish a solid foundation, just like the Root Chakra provides. This grounding exercise will help you connect with the Earth's energy and create stability for your manifestations:

Root Chakra Grounding Exercise

Find a quiet, peaceful outdoor space or a room where you can sit comfortably.

Sit with your back straight and your feet flat on the ground.

Close your eyes and take several deep breaths, inhaling and exhaling slowly.

Visualize roots extending from the base of your spine and your feet, reaching deep into the Earth's core.

Imagine these roots anchoring you firmly to the Earth, like the roots of a tree.

Feel the Earth's energy rising through these roots, filling you with a sense of security and stability.

- Affirm to yourself: "I am grounded, safe, and secure. I am ready to manifest my desires."
- Spend a few moments in this grounded state, feeling the Earth's energy supporting you.
- When you're ready, slowly open your eyes and proceed with your manifestation work.

Grounding is essential for bringing your manifestations into the physical realm, just as a tree needs strong roots to grow tall and flourish.

In the next chapter, we will explore the power of affirmations and journaling in the manifestation process. These practices will help you maintain focus and clarity on your desires.

Continue your journey by exploring affirmations and journaling in Chapter 5 of the workbook.

Chapter Five
Affirmations and Journaling

Welcome to Chapter 5 of your Witch Pu$$y Manifestation journey. In this chapter, we'll delve into the power of affirmations and journaling as essential tools to maintain focus and clarity on your desires. These practices will help you nurture and manifest your intentions with the creative energy of your Sacral Chakra.

5.1
DAILY AFFIRMATIONS

Affirmations are positive statements that reinforce your beliefs and intentions. When used consistently, they have the power to reprogram your mind and align your energy with your desires. Here's how to create and practice daily affirmations:

Creating Effective Affirmations

Begin with a clear intention. What do you want to manifest? Be specific and concise.

Transform your intention into a positive, present-tense statement. For example, if your intention is to find a loving relationship, your affirmation could be: "I am attracting a loving and fulfilling relationship into my life."

Make your affirmations personal and emotionally charged. Use words and phrases that resonate with you deeply.

Practicing Daily Affirmations:

Set aside a specific time each day to repeat your affirmations. Mornings or evenings work well, but choose a time that suits your routine.

Stand or sit in a relaxed and comfortable position.

Close your eyes and take a few deep breaths to center yourself.

Repeat your affirmations with conviction and belief. Visualize your desires as already fulfilled and feel the emotions associated with them. Feel the leather seats of your new car. Smell the fresh cut grass outside of your dream home.

Repeat each affirmation several times. You can use the same affirmation or focus on a different one each day.

Trust that your affirmations are working to align your energy with your desires.

EXERCISE 5.1:
DAILY AFFIRMATIONS

Create a list of daily affirmations that align with your manifestations. Be sure to include affirmations related to your healing and the specific desires you wish to manifest. Here are a few examples to get you started:

- "I am worthy of love, happiness, and abundance."
- "I release the past and embrace my healed self."
- "I trust my intuition and make choices that serve my highest good."
- "I manifest my desires with ease and joy."

Repeat these affirmations daily, and as you do, believe in your power to manifest your intentions.

5.2
MANIFESTATION JOURNAL

Journaling is a powerful practice for tracking your progress, recording synchronicities, and expressing gratitude for your manifestations. Your journal is a sacred space for your manifestation journey. Here's how to create and use a manifestation journal:

CREATING YOUR MANIFESTATION JOURNAL

1. Choose a journal or notebook that resonates with you. It could be plain or decorative; the choice is personal. I have, however, provided pages in the back of this workbook for you to journal and complete exercises.

2. Dedicate this journal exclusively to your manifestation work.

Using Your Manifestation Journal

1. Begin each journal entry with the date.

2. Write down your daily affirmations and intentions.

3. Record any thoughts, feelings, or synchronicities related to your manifestations. Be specific and descriptive.

4. Express gratitude for the manifestations that have already occurred or any progress you've made.

5. Use your journal as a space for self-reflection and self-care. Write about your healing journey, challenges, and breakthroughs.

EXERCISE 5.2: MANIFESTATION JOURNALING

Set aside a few minutes each day to journal about your manifestation journey. Write about your experiences, thoughts, and feelings related to your affirmations and manifestations. Remember to express gratitude for every step of your journey.

Your journal serves as a record of your growth and progress, helping you stay connected to your desires and your healing process.

In the next chapter, we will explore rituals and candle magic as additional tools to enhance your manifestation abilities and strengthen your connection to the divine feminine energy within you.

Continue your journey by exploring rituals and candle magic in Chapter 6 of the workbook.

Chapter Six
Rituals and Candle Magic

Welcome to Chapter 6 of your Witch Pu$$y Manifestation journey. In this chapter, we'll explore the use of rituals and candle magic to enhance your manifestation abilities and strengthen your connection to the divine feminine energy within you. These practices can amplify your intentions and bring an extra layer of power to your manifestations.

6.1
CANDLE MAGIC RITUAL

Candle magic is a potent form of manifestation that taps into the element of fire. Fire represents transformation and the swift manifestation of desires. Here's a simple candle magic ritual to get you started:

CANDLE MAGIC RITUAL

1. For this ritual, we will be using the Witch Pu$$y manifestation candle that you should have purchased with this book. If you did not, no worries!

You can choose a candle that resonates with your manifestation goals. Different colors are associated with various intentions. For example:

Red for passion and love

Green for abundance and prosperity

Blue for communication and truth

Pink for self-love and healing

White for purity and clarity

2. Find a quiet, undisturbed space to perform your ritual. Place the candle on a stable surface.

3. Sit comfortably in front of the candle, take a few deep breaths, and focus on your intention. Visualize your desire as if it's already happening.

4. Light the candle, and as you do, say a simple affirmation related to your intention. For example, if you're manifesting love, you could say, "I am open to receiving love and affection."

5. Gaze at the candle flame, and let its energy fill you with positivity and determination. Feel the energy of your intention infusing the flame.

6. Spend as much time as you like meditating on your intention. Visualize it in detail, imagining how it feels to have it manifest in your life.

7. When you feel ready, extinguish the candle, either by blowing it out gently or using a snuffer. As you do, say, "So it is. It is done. Asé"

8. Trust that your intention has been released into the universe, and the candle's flame has carried your desire into the realms of manifestation.

9. Repeat this ritual regularly, perhaps during significant phases of the moon or when you feel the need to recharge your intention.

6.2
FULL MOON RELEASE RITUAL

The full moon is a potent time for releasing what no longer serves you and making space for your manifestations. This ritual harnesses the energy of the full moon to clear the path for your desires:

Full Moon Release Ritual

1. Check the lunar calendar to find the date of the next full moon.

2. On the evening of the full moon, find a quiet, outdoor space where you can see the moon clearly. Alternatively, you can perform this ritual near a window with a view of the moon.

3. Sit or stand comfortably and take a few deep breaths to center yourself.

4. Gaze at the full moon and say aloud or in your mind, "I release what no longer serves me. I am ready to make space for my manifestations."

5. Close your eyes and visualize any emotional wounds, limiting beliefs, or obstacles that are blocking your manifestations.

6. Imagine these obstacles as heavy stones or burdens and visualize releasing them one by one into the moon's radiant light.

7. As you release each burden, affirm to yourself, "I release and let go. I am free to manifest my desires."

8. Spend as much time as you need in this releasing meditation.

9. When you're ready, open your eyes and offer gratitude to the moon for its assistance in your releasing process.

10. Trust that you've cleared the way for your manifestations to unfold.

Both candle magic and full moon rituals are powerful tools to amplify your intentions and connect with the divine feminine energy within you. Incorporate these practices into your manifestation journey as needed, and watch as your desires begin to take shape.

In the final chapter of this workbook, we'll discuss the importance of self-care, self-love, and celebrating your successes as you continue on your path to manifestation.

Continue your journey by exploring self-care and self-love in Chapter 7 of the workbook.

Chapter Seven
Embracing Your Journey

Welcome to Chapter 7, the final chapter of your Witch Pu$$y Manifestation journey. In this chapter, we'll explore the importance of self-care, self-love, and celebrating your successes as you continue on your path to manifestation.

7.1
SELF-CARE AND SELF-LOVE

As you progress on your manifestation journey, it's crucial to prioritize self-care and self-love. These practices not only nurture your well-being but also strengthen your connection to your divine feminine energy, enhancing your manifestation abilities.

SELF-CARE PRACTICES

1. Meditation: Regular meditation helps you stay centered and aligned with your intentions.

2. Physical Health: Nourish your body with wholesome food, exercise, and adequate rest. A healthy body supports a clear mind.

3. Nature Connection: Spend time in nature to recharge and reconnect with the Earth's energy.

4. Creativity: Engage in creative pursuits that feed your soul, such as art, music, or writing.

5. Rest and Relaxation: Set aside time for relaxation and pampering. A relaxed mind is more receptive to manifestations.

SELF-LOVE PRACTICES

1. Positive Self-Talk: Replace self-criticism with self-compassion. Speak to yourself kindly and encourage yourself as you would a dear friend.

2. Forgiveness: Forgive yourself for past mistakes and perceived shortcomings. Forgiveness is a powerful act of self-love and healing.

3. Affirmations: Use self-love affirmations to reinforce your self-worth and deservingness of your manifestations.

4. Gratitude: Express gratitude for yourself and your journey. Gratitude amplifies positive energy.

7.2
CELEBRATING YOUR SUCCESSES

As you progress on your manifestation journey, take the time to acknowledge and celebrate your successes, no matter how small. Celebrating your achievements reinforces your belief in your manifesting abilities and keeps your energy aligned with your goals.

CELEBRATION IDEAS:

Journaling: Write about your achievements and the positive changes you've experienced since beginning your journey.

Rituals: Create rituals to mark significant milestones in your manifestations, such as lighting a special candle or performing a gratitude ritual.

Self-Care Treats: Treat yourself to something special, whether it's a spa day, a favorite meal, or a day of relaxation.

Share with Others: Share your successes with trusted friends or loved ones who support your journey. Their encouragement can be uplifting.

Visualization: Visualize your next steps and the even greater successes that await you. Keep your vision alive and vibrant.

Remember that the journey of manifestation is as much about self-discovery and growth as it is about manifesting tangible desires. Embrace your journey with love, patience, and an open heart.

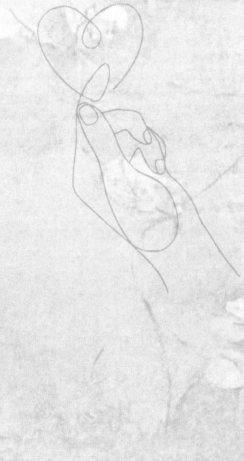

Conclusion

Congratulations on completing the Witch Pu$$y Manifestation Workbook! You've embarked on a transformative journey to harness your divine feminine energy, heal from past traumas, and manifest the life you've envisioned. Your journey doesn't end here. It's a lifelong path of self-discovery and growth.

Embrace self-care and self-love as ongoing practices, nurturing your well-being and strengthening your connection to your divine feminine energy. Celebrate each step of your journey and trust that you are a powerful creator.

May your path be filled with love, abundance, and fulfillment. Keep manifesting your dreams and sharing your unique light with the world.

Stay empowered and continue embracing your divine feminine energy as you manifest the life you desire!

Continue your journey into confidence and self-love by utilizing the worksheets in the following pages to help you become equipped to create the best version of YOU! Thank you for taking a bet on the forever winning piece.... YOU!

With Love,

— *Spicy Red*

Vision Board

PROFESSIONAL GOALS	PERSONAL GOALS

HEALTH GOALS	FINANCIAL GOALS

RELATIONSHIP GOALS	BIG DREAMS

HOBBIES	NOTES

My Version of Success

What does success mean to you? Be as specific as you can!

_____
_____
_____
_____
_____
_____

Which steps do you need to take to get there?

What does it feel like after you've finally made it?

_____
_____
_____
_____
_____
_____

Money Flows To Me

Write your dreams on the leaves: Which things will you be able to afford when you have all the money you need?

Lovers, Friends, Family

What needs to change in your relationships?

_____
_____
_____
_____
_____

You've now got the social life you always hoped for. What is it like?

_____
_____
_____
_____
_____
_____
_____
_____

Act as if it already happened...

Name your dream	Why is it important to you?

What will it be like when the dream has come true? How does it feel?

_____

_____

_____

_____

_____

_____

_____

_____

_____

The Future Me

What will you look like and how will you feel when you have the life you desire? What has changed in your mental state, environment and/or physical appearance?

_____
_____
_____
_____
_____
_____
_____
_____
_____
_____
_____
_____
_____
_____

Take Inspired Action

After visualization, it is time for inspired action. It is a key component of manifestation because hopes and dreams alone won't change your life.

You have to take the steps to change it. Inspired action aligns your energy and vibration with the universe and allows you to co-create with the universe to bring your desires into reality.

When you take inspired action, you are signaling to the universe that you are ready to receive what you have asked for and you are taking the necessary steps to bring it into your reality. It helps you to build momentum towards your goals and creates a sense of empowerment and confidence in your ability to manifest what you desire.

Manifest Your Timeline

To manifest a new reality, you need to know what you want. Create your 5-year-plan with the help of the questions below.

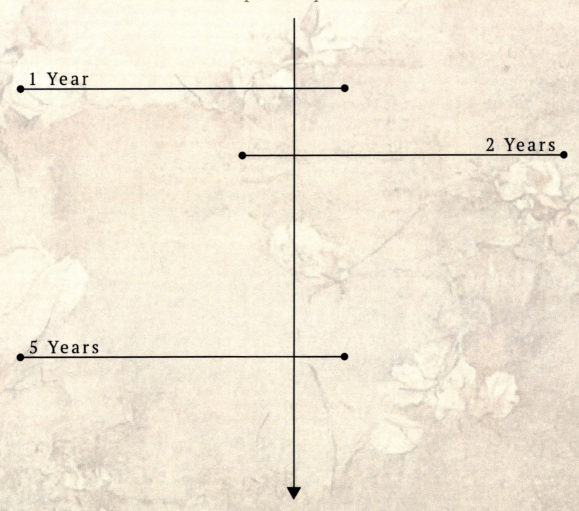

QUESTIONS TO GET YOU STARTED:
Where do you live? What have you accomplished? What do your days look like?
What kind of job/education you have? Who is in your life?
Which of your current problems have you left behind?

Find Your Ikigai

What job, business idea, project or endeavor fits in the intersection of the circles?

That is most likely your true purpose, or ikigai, as the Japanese call it.

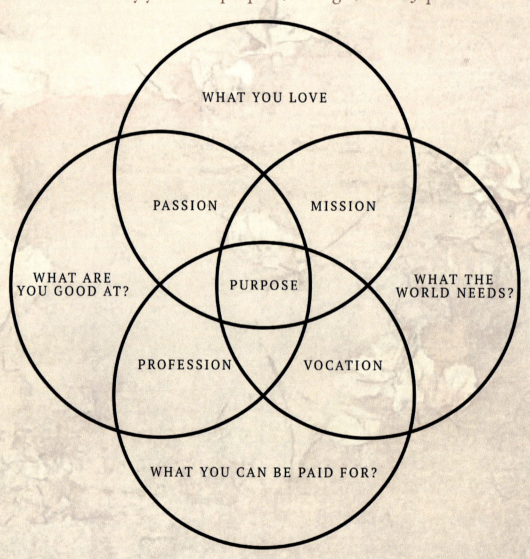

My Happy Schedule

Practicing self-care raises your vibration and attracts abundance into your life. How do you want to feel on a daily basis? What are the little things you can do everyday to feel more joy?

MY PERFECT MORNING ROUTINE
_____
_____
_____
_____
_____
_____
_____

SELF CARE

PERSONAL TIME

MINDFULNESS EXERCISES TO TRY
_____
_____
_____
_____
_____
_____
_____
_____

Identify Limiting Beliefs

First write down beliefs about anything you feel strongly about and that influence your daily life. Then you can reflect which ones might be holding you back from creating the life you truly want.

MY BELIEFS
(money, relationships, work, love, studies, etc.)

Which beliefs help me to grow and which ones might be limiting me?

_____
_____
_____
_____

Challenge Limiting Beliefs

Limiting Belief 1: _____

Is this belief really grounded? Is it helping me to progress towards my dreams?
_____
_____

Reframe It: How could I challenge this belief?
_____
_____
_____

Limiting Belief 2: _____

Is this belief really grounded? Is it helping me to progress towards my dreams?
_____
_____

Reframe It: How could I challenge this belief?
_____
_____
_____

Money Blocks

Identify the mental blocks you have with money and create a positive affirmation to reframe it.

MONEY BLOCK	POSITIVE AFFIRMATION

Release Your Past

Are there experiences, memories and thoughts that have been haunting you and pulling you down? It's time to approach those memories with self-compassion and acceptance.

MEMORY/EXPERIENCE

What can you say to forgive yourself and to accept the past?

_____
_____
_____
_____
_____
_____
_____
_____
_____
_____

Affirmations for when the memory comes back to bother you.

_____
_____
_____
_____
_____
_____
_____
_____
_____
_____

Daily Gratitude

TODAY I ACHIEVED...

DAILY GRATITUDE LIST

THINGS THAT MADE ME HAPPY:

INTENTION FOR TOMORROW:

NOTE TO SELF

_____
_____
_____
_____
_____

Daily Gratitude

TODAY I ACHIEVED...

THINGS THAT MADE ME HAPPY:

DAILY GRATITUDE LIST

INTENTION FOR TOMORROW:

NOTE TO SELF

_____
_____
_____
_____
_____

Daily Gratitude

TODAY I ACHIEVED...

THINGS THAT MADE ME HAPPY:

DAILY GRATITUDE LIST

INTENTION FOR TOMORROW:

NOTE TO SELF

Daily Gratitude

TODAY I ACHIEVED...

DAILY GRATITUDE LIST

THINGS THAT MADE ME HAPPY:

INTENTION FOR TOMORROW:

NOTE TO SELF

_____
_____
_____
_____
_____
_____

Daily Gratitude

TODAY I ACHIEVED...

DAILY GRATITUDE LIST

THINGS THAT MADE ME HAPPY:

INTENTION FOR TOMORROW:

NOTE TO SELF

_____
_____
_____
_____
_____

Daily Gratitude

TODAY I ACHIEVED...

DAILY GRATITUDE LIST

THINGS THAT MADE ME HAPPY:

INTENTION FOR TOMORROW:

NOTE TO SELF

Daily Gratitude

TODAY I ACHIEVED...

DAILY GRATITUDE LIST

THINGS THAT MADE ME HAPPY:

INTENTION FOR TOMORROW:

NOTE TO SELF

_____
_____
_____
_____
_____
_____

Weekly Gratitude

THE BEST THING THAT HAPPENED THIS WEEK

THINGS I LOVE ABOUT MYSELF

_____
_____
_____
_____
_____
_____
_____
_____
_____

PEOPLE I'M GRATEFUL FOR

THINGS I LOOK FORWARD TO

THINGS THAT MAKE ME HAPPY

Weekly Gratitude

THE BEST THING THAT HAPPENED THIS WEEK

THINGS I LOVE ABOUT MYSELF
_____
_____
_____
_____
_____
_____
_____
_____

PEOPLE I'M GRATEFUL FOR

THINGS I LOOK FORWARD TO

THINGS THAT MAKE ME HAPPY

Weekly Gratitude

THE BEST THING THAT HAPPENED THIS WEEK

THINGS I LOVE ABOUT MYSELF

PEOPLE I'M GRATEFUL FOR

THINGS I LOOK FORWARD TO

THINGS THAT MAKE ME HAPPY

Weekly Gratitude

THE BEST THING THAT HAPPENED THIS WEEK

THINGS I LOVE ABOUT MYSELF

_____
_____
_____
_____
_____
_____
_____
_____

PEOPLE I'M GRATEFUL FOR

THINGS I LOOK FORWARD TO

THINGS THAT MAKE ME HAPPY

This Month's Gratitude Page

Write down the things that made you feel grateful in the last month.

BLESSINGS	OPPORTUNITIES

PEOPLE & THINGS	CHALLENGES

This Month's Gratitude Page

Write down the things that made you feel grateful in the last month.

BLESSINGS	OPPORTUNITIES

PEOPLE & THINGS	CHALLENGES

This Month's Gratitude Page

Write down the things that made you feel grateful in the last month.

BLESSINGS	OPPORTUNITIES

PEOPLE & THINGS	CHALLENGES

Self-Love Affirmations

Affirmations for getting through difficult moments

_____
_____
_____
_____

Affirmations for loving my body

_____
_____
_____
_____

Affirmations for believing in myself

_____
_____
_____
_____

Abundance Affirmations

Affirmations for manifesting money

_____
_____
_____
_____

Affirmations for manifesting love

_____
_____
_____
_____

Affirmations for manifesting all my dreams to come true

_____
_____
_____
_____
_____

Life Goal Affirmations

Affirmations for believing my goals will come true

_____

_____

_____

_____

Affirmations for strength on my path

_____

_____

_____

_____

Affirmations for having the support and resources I need

_____

_____

_____

_____

Affirmations For Receiving Love

Affirmations for believing I'm worthy of love

_____
_____
_____
_____

Affirmations for manifesting love into my life

_____
_____
_____
_____

Affirmations for knowing that love is endless, not scarce

_____
_____
_____
_____

Journal Prompt 1

Journal Prompt 2

Journal Prompt 3

Journal Prompt 4

Journal Prompt 5

Journal Prompt 6

Journal Prompt 7

Journal Prompt 8

Journal Prompt 9

Journal Prompt 10

Author Bio

Spicy Red is a remarkable nurse-turned-entrepreneur who has harnessed her nurturing spirit and creativity to empower women in their journey of self-discovery and manifestation. With a background in nursing and a passion for holistic well-being, she's emerged as a visionary in the realm of personal growth and healing.

As a dedicated mother and successful entrepreneur, Spicy Red understands the demands of modern life and the importance of balancing one's physical and emotional well-being. Her journey of self-discovery led her to create a groundbreaking series of digital manifestation and mental health workbooks, tailored to women seeking to unlock their divine feminine energy and manifest their deepest desires.

Her best-selling product, the 'Witch Pu$$y' manifestation bundle, has garnered praise for its innovative approach to using the sacral and root chakras in conjunction with candle magic to amplify intentions. This unique offering has resonated with women worldwide, igniting their inner fires and guiding them on a path of self-empowerment.

With a vision beyond her current successes, Spicy Red plans to expand her offerings further. She envisions a future where holistic well-being is accessible to all, and where her expertise in nurturing the mind, body, and spirit leads to even more transformative products and services.

Unleash Your Power with the Witch Pu$$y Manifestation Workbook

Dive deep into the magic of manifestation with the Witch Pu$$y Manifestation Workbook, a transformative guide designed to awaken the divine feminine energy within you. This workbook is not just a tool; it's a journey through the realms of self-discovery, empowerment, and cosmic connection. With each page, you'll unlock secrets to harnessing your inner witch, channeling the potent energy that resides within your very core.

What You Will Discover:

Unlock Your Manifestation Magic: Learn the art of setting intentions that resonate with the universe, creating a flow of abundance and fulfillment in your life.

Balance and Align Your Chakras: Dive into powerful exercises and rituals that open and align your energy centers, enhancing your vibrational frequency and spiritual connectivity.

Embrace Your Divine Feminine: Explore practices that celebrate your sensuality, creativity, and emotional intelligence, empowering you to embrace your full potential.

Transformative Rituals and Spells: Engage in thoughtfully crafted rituals and spells that elevate your manifestation abilities, guiding you to manifest your desires with precision and power.

Cultivate Self-Love and Confidence: Build a profound relationship with yourself through exercises designed to boost self-esteem and self-worth, laying the foundation for successful manifestation.

The Witch Pu$$y Manifestation Workbook is your invitation to step into a life where dreams and reality merge. Whether you're a seasoned practitioner or new to the path of witchcraft, this workbook offers a unique blend of ancient wisdom and modern manifestation techniques, all designed to empower you to live a life of abundance, joy, and magic.

Are you ready to embrace your inner witch and transform your dreams into reality? Let the Witch Pu$$y Manifestation Workbook guide you through a journey of empowerment, magic, and manifestation.

Made in the USA
Middletown, DE
13 May 2024

54248111R00046